WORLD WAR II CARTOONS
OF AKRON'S
WEB BROWN

TIM CARROLL

THE
History
PRESS

Published by The History Press
Charleston, SC
www.historypress.com

Copyright © 2020 by Tim Carroll
All rights reserved

Cover images reprinted with permission of the
Akron Beacon Journal and Ohio.com.

First published 2020

Manufactured in the United States

ISBN 9781467146258

Library of Congress Control Number: 2020932881

CONTENTS

INTRODUCTION

One of the best cartoonists of the World War II era was Web Brown, who worked for the *Akron Beacon Journal* from 1929 until he retired at age 69 on Christmas Eve, 1945. Web began his 46-year career as a cartoonist in 1899 after returning from the Spanish-American War. Web loved art growing up and decided to be a cartoonist—despite having no experience or formal training. He followed the rule that if you worked hard and loved something, you could be successful. When he told his family that he planned to pursue his dream of being a cartoonist, they laughed at him. Web told the *Beacon Journal* for his retirement article published December 23, 1945, "I always wanted to be a cartoonist when I was a boy, but I never attended art school. Everything I got came the hard way. People used to tell me: 'It's born in you'. But I say it's not born in you. You have to like a thing well enough to stick to it long enough."

Web was inspired and mentored by Akron-born cartoonist Charles Nelan, whose cartoons for the *New York Herald* brought him national recognition in the late 1890s. Nelan, who was the first syndicated cartoonist in the country, later worked for the *Philadelphia North American* and *New York Globe* before dying of tuberculosis in 1904 at age forty-five. Most Akronites don't know that Nelan, one of the greatest cartoonists of his time, is buried in the St. Vincent Cemetery at the intersection of Merriman Road and West Market Street next to Tangier restaurant in Akron. "I will never quit until I become the equal of Charles Nelan. It's in me, and I know it," said Web in the July 17, 1909, *Akron Beacon Journal*, when asked about the influence Nelan had on him.

Web was highly sought after early in his career working for papers in Akron, Cleveland, Canton, Youngstown, and even being enticed to go out to Boston. An article in the *Youngstown Vindicator* on October 9, 1902, proclaimed that Web

> has accepted a position with the Boston Post, and has gone to the hub of culture and beans. Brown is young, but is one of the very best cartoonists in the country, his best work comparing favorably with that in the cartoon papers in New York and Chicago. There are men today doing art work in his line in Chicago and making good money who can't touch him with a 10-foot pole. Brown does what few cartoonists do he draws carefully, apparently holding that what is worth doing is worth doing well.

Web was born January 28, 1876, in Akron and raised by his father and grandparents after his mother died when he was 18 months old. He attended Jennings High School on Summit Street and Buchtel College for a year. When Web was 16, he attended a local military meeting at Assembly Hall which was the Armory in 1892. He ended up joining the Army even though his grandma had told him he was not allowed to do so. Of getting into this experience, Web recollected,

> Captain Conger came over to me just before the company was formed for drill and asked me if I was interested in military work. I told him I'd like to enlist but I was only 16 years old. He sized me up and said, 'You are tall enough to pass for 18' which was the age limit, and no one would know the difference. Before I knew it I had signed up for three years and started to drill that very night.

Web was married in 1897, and in 1898 he headed off to Cuba to fight in the Spanish-American War, during which he reached the rank of sergeant major. Web was part of Company B in the 8th Ohio Volunteer Infantry. They served under Lieutenant Colonel Charles Dick, a fellow Akronite. Dick, who later became a US senator, has a street named after him in Akron's Highland Square neighborhood. Ohio's 8th Regiment, which included Akron's Company B, lost 72 men during the Spanish-American War even though they did not fire a single shot.

Web had over 30 years of experience and had been known as one of the best cartoonists in the country since the early 1900s when he made the best cartoons of his career during the World War II era. Web produced cartoons that reflected his sense of humor, history, and justice all while puffing on his daily cigar. The *Beacon Journal* was one of the best newspapers in the country, with an award-winning editorial page led by their legendary editor John S. Knight. Knight and his staff consistently put out top notch editorials, and it was Web Brown's job to put out excellent political cartoons to accompany them. The *Beacon Journal* editors commented on his final day of work:

> Web Brown has enabled the Beacon Journal to rank with the nation's leading newspapers in the important matter of editorial page cartoons. And it is an important matter, for surveys show that even the most hurried readers take the time to absorb the message conveyed by the cartoon.

When Web Brown retired on Christmas Eve of 1945, a few months after the surrender of the Japanese, it was like his war had ended, too. It seemed like Web had waited to retire until the war was over. Web stayed active all the way up to his death at age 98 on March 4, 1974. The Peninsula Library has a painting Web did for them of the canal that is dated 1972, which means he painted it and gave it to them when he was 96 years old. Web is buried in Glendale Cemetery on the edge of downtown Akron. If you pull in the cemetery entrance and take the first driveway on the left you will find Web's grave at the top of the hill in section 21.

The cartoons that follow tell the story of World War II with over 200 of Web Brown's outstanding cartoons in chronological order from 1934 through 1945.

Unless otherwise noted, all images are reprinted with permission of the *Akron Beacon Journal* and Ohio.com.

One

WAR BREWS IN EUROPE

1934–1936

Question Over Austria

JULY 27, 1934.
The world watches as Hitler and the Nazis attempt to overthrow the Austrian government in July 1934. The attempted Putsch was started when the Nazis assassinated the leader of Austria, Engelbert Dollfuss. Hitler's future ally, Benito Mussolini, comes to the aid of Austria. Mussolini will later jump on the Hitler bandwagon thinking that the German dictator will win World War II.

JULY 28, 1934. Death returns to Austria as rebel Nazi forces are routed in what is called a civil war. Thousands are said to have died in the clashes. The rebellion is put down and the Nazis are defeated. Austria survives for now, but in the coming years Hitler will succeed in taking Austria.

JANUARY 29, 1935. Debate rages in the United States as the Roosevelt Administration looks to join the World Court. America rejected joining the League of Nations after seeing Wilson's Fourteen Points brushed aside at the Versailles Peace Conference in Paris after World War I. Americans do not want another war and they figure the best way to avoid it is to stay out of European politics.

JANUARY 30, 1935. The US Senate voted 52 for joining the World Court and 36 against, which was just shy of the two-thirds majority needed for approval. Controversial Catholic priest Charles Coughlin, who used his radio show based in Detroit to help defeat the bill, touted the 200,000 telegrams his followers sent to Congress in an effort to keep the United States out of the World Court.

AUGUST 22, 1935. Long remembering John Bull (Great Britain) dragging them into World War I, America is determined to stay out of the war they see festering in Europe and East Africa. The Senate passed the first Neutrality Act placing an embargo on the shipment of arms, munitions, and implements of war to belligerent nations and banning American citizens from traveling on ships of nations at war.

AUGUST 23, 1935. The US House of Representatives, with guidance from President Roosevelt, debates the Neutrality Act that will pass August 31, 1935. Americans heeded George Washington's advice in his farewell address to stay out of European conflicts. America found themselves with 21,000 new millionaires from the spoils of World War I. They wanted to make sure such a tragedy never happens again.

SEPTEMBER 4, 1935. Benito Mussolini is encouraged to continue his conquest of Ethiopia by mimicking Japan's aggressive actions in China and Hitler's rearming of his military in direct violation of the Treaty of Versailles. The League of Nations is powerless to stop them.

SEPTEMBER 25, 1935. Benito Mussolini refuses to discuss the status of Ethiopia before the League of Nations. Mussolini had a habit of picking on smaller countries and became infamous for having trouble defeating them. In this case, he has to worry about how the British will respond to his act of aggression.

OCTOBER 10, 1935. The Treaty of Versailles from the start had the world on a trajectory toward a second world war. Italy, Japan, and Germany are all demanding more land and resources for their struggling populations during the Great Depression. Distracted, England prefers to have Uncle Sam deal with Japan while they protect their interests and the various dictators take advantage of each other's aggression to make gains.

MARCH 9, 1936. Hitler ignores another provision of the Treaty of Versailles and sends his troops in the demilitarized Rhineland. France responds by sending troops to her eastern border while Britain signals they will do nothing to stop Hitler. Once again, the United States wishes there was a just peace following World War I.

Another Scrap Of Paper

And So They Voted Nazi

MARCH 30, 1936. An election is held in Germany, and Adolf Hitler receives nearly 45 million votes, or 97 percent of the vote. Hitler and the Nazis had never won more than 40 percent of the vote when Germany was a parliamentary democracy, including the 1932 election where he first came to power. Now, with a bayonet at their back, the German people vote for the only candidate on the ballot.

11

JUNE 15, 1936. On behalf the War Department, Senator Bennett Clark of Missouri introduced a bill that gives the military complete control of the country with censorship of the press, drafting of all men over the age of 18, suspension of the right of habeas corpus and a jury trial, seizure of any property by the government, and regulation of food and commodities.

Two

Boots on the Ground
1937–August 31, 1939

Easter Comes To Europe

WE B. BROWN

March 27, 1937. Easter in 1937 is overshadowed by the coming war in Europe.

The Best Argument Against War

KILLED in REVOLUTIONARY WAR · KILLED CIVIL WAR · KILLED SPANISH AMERICAN WAR · KILLED WORLD WAR · RESERVED FOR FUTURE WARS

WEB.BROWN

MAY 31, 1937. Memorial Day 1937 is celebrated with a reminder of the steep price paid in human life for each war that had been fought in the United States thus far. American veterans from the Civil War, Spanish-American War, and the First World War had no love for the bloodshed and loathed the loss of young lives.

JULY 5, 1937. Uncle Sam's Constitutional Democracy, established in 1776, finds itself under attack by antidemocratic world forces. The Articles of Confederation were replaced by the Constitution in 1789. America, like most fledgling democracies, always faced threats to its existence from the War of 1812 to the bloody Civil War in the 1860s. Uncle Sam continues to protect the foundations of democracy in hopes of a more peaceful world.

Watch The Waters, Uncle

THE FOUNDING FATHERS

HOW'M I DOING BOYS?

UNCLE SAM

ANTI-DEMOCRATIC WORLD FORCES

CONSTITUTIONAL DEMOCRACY
DEDICATED JULY 4, 1776
ESTABLISHED MARCH 4, 1789

WEB.BROWN

SEPTEMBER 22, 1937.
Japan bombs Nanking as the undeclared Sino-Japanese War in China continues. Secretary Hull sends Ambassador Leland Harrison of Switzerland to Geneva to meet with The League of Nations on the matter. The United States watches cautiously as they know Britain and France want their help with Japan and Americans are weary of going to war to protect French and British interests in China.

SEPTEMBER 27, 1937.
Mussolini and Hitler meet at the Berlin Conference. The United States is not fooled by Hitler and Mussolini's claims of wanting world peace. In the years to come, Hitler and Mussolini are expected to continue rearmament as the dictators look to expand and make land grabs.

15

A New Fling At World Saving

THOSE ARE NOBLE SENTIMENTS, BUT HAVE YOU FORGOTTEN WHAT HAPPENED IN 1917?

F.D.R.

CHICAGO ANTI-WAR ADDRESS

— WE B. BROWN —

OCTOBER 7, 1937. President Roosevelt gives his famous speech directed at Germany, Italy, and Japan calling for the quarantine of aggressors. The British and French leaders celebrate what they see as America coming in on their side while the aggressor nations brush aside the speech. Germany told Roosevelt he was headed for the shipwreck that was 1917. The United States also joins the League of Nations in condemning Japanese treaty violations.

Another World Series

OCTOBER 8, 1937. October is time for the World Series, and in 1939 Mars and death have gotten in on the action. It seems the Earth is headed for another war with even more deaths than during World War I. Veterans of that war know the horrors of war and want no part of round two.

OCTOBER 25, 1937. Norman Davis heads overseas to attend the Brussels Peace Conference, where Britain and France have gone from condemning Mussolini and Hitler's acts in Spain to praising them. General Franco's rebel army, backed by Hitler and Mussolini, is on the verge of winning in Spain, and there is no sign France and Britain want to quarantine the aggressors after FDR's speech.

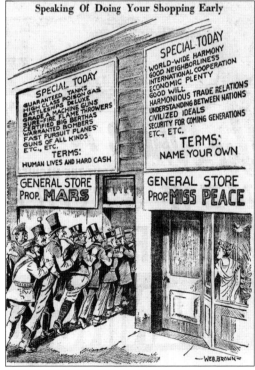

DECEMBER 3, 1937. It's Christmas season, and Mars is doing plenty of business while lady peace could use some customers. The nations of the world, including Uncle Sam, prefer to stock up on weapons of war rather than invest in principles of peace.

The Naval Race And The Finish Line

THE SECOND WORLD WAR

JANUARY 25, 1938. President Roosevelt is in the process of building the biggest navy in American history while claiming to hate war and love peace. The other nations of the world all do the same thing.

FEBRUARY 9, 1938. Americans see President Roosevelt leading them down the same path paved by Woodrow Wilson in 1917. Noting that an agreement existed—an agreement the British House of Commons had no knowledge of and that led to Britain's involvement in World War I—Senator Hiram Johnson insists that the state department clarify if any secret agreements exist between America and other nations.

Is History Being Repeated?

MARCH 7, 1938. Joseph Stalin continues his trials of old Bolsheviks with the same routine, hysterical, phony, coerced confessions of treason designed to eliminate anyone who might dare to challenge him. Forced labor, death camps, and concentration camps show Stalin has much in common with Hitler. Stalin will be an ally in World War II and an enemy of the United States immediately after.

MARCH 12, 1938. Chancellor Schuschnigg of Austria cancels his planned vote on Austrian independence as Hitler amasses troops at the border, forcing his resignation. Nazi troops enter Austria and quickly put their people under the heel of the brutal Nazi regime. Chancellor Schuschnigg is arrested, and Hitler will spend years humiliating him in a German concentration camp. Unlike Hitler, however, Schuschnigg survives World War II and will live until 1977.

The Woodchopper Of Doorn Remembers

TWENTY-FOUR YEARS AGO I THOUGHT I COULD GET AWAY WITH ANYTHING, TOO!

EX-KAISER WILHELM

HITLER ON THE MARCH

HOLLAND

—WEB.BROWN—

MARCH 14, 1934. The memory of Ex-Kaiser Wilhelm, who led Germany to war in 1914, is invoked. Hitler, like Wilhelm, has dreams of a great German empire. Wilhelm brought destruction to Germany, and Hitler will bring complete destruction.

Heil Hitler!

AUSTRIAN SUICIDES

—WEB.BROWN—

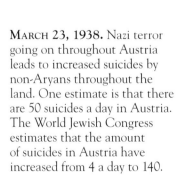

MARCH 23, 1938. Nazi terror going on throughout Austria leads to increased suicides by non-Aryans throughout the land. One estimate is that there are 50 suicides a day in Austria. The World Jewish Congress estimates that the amount of suicides in Austria have increased from 4 a day to 140.

APRIL 11, 1938. Hitler holds a plebiscite, or vote, on whether Nazi Germany should take over Austria. As is typical, the Nazis get well over 48 million "yes" votes out of 50 million registered voters—99 percent of the vote. Austria's fate is officially sealed and lies in a coffin.

The Last Nail In The Coffin

The World's An Easter Egg

APRIL 16, 1938. Mars does some Easter egg decorating. The god of war paints his egg with the four symbols doing the devil's work across the world this holiday season. Mussolini, Hitler, Japan, and Stalin are all represented. Dictators can't always be friends, and democracies have always been willing to make deals with the devil. Stalin, ironically, will be a United States ally during World War II.

Capitol Hill Gets A Petition

WE'VE BEEN THROUGH WAR! WE KNOW WHAT IT MEANS!

CONGRESS

VETERANS OF FOREIGN WARS

KEEP AMERICA OUT OF WAR
3,640,890
SIGNERS FROM EVERY STATE

—WEB.BROWN—

APRIL 29, 1938. Congress gets a powerful petition from a drive led by the Veterans of Foreign Wars. More than three million signatures were collected by the Veterans of Foreign Wars, who were aided by church groups, businesses, and women's peace organizations. Part of the reason for the petition was the recent bills introduced in Congress on conscription and what would amount to a military dictatorship.

For The Moment—Maybe

THE NEW BELT MAKES IT WORK BETTER, BENITO!

EUROPE

HITLER'S VISIT TO ROME

HITLER   MUSSOLINI

AXIS

ROME BERLIN

—WEB.BROWN—

MAY 4, 1938. Hitler visits Mussolini in Rome, and the two best friends spend the day laying wreaths at various graves and carrying on together. The Rome–Berlin Axis seems to be running fine despite a British–Italian Pact made just two weeks prior.

MAY 11, 1938. Great Britain, a week after Hitler showed them up in Rome, is still touting the Easter Accords made with Mussolini. Britain shows once again that they are more than willing to sacrifice other small nations to protect their own interests. They officially recognize Ethiopia as part of the Italian Empire to the League of Nations. This reminds America that the British embrace is not for friendship but as a way to stab their friends in the back.

AUGUST 31, 1938. Hitler has his eyes on Czechoslovakia, and even the voice of Kaiser Wilhelm whispering to him from exile in Doorn cannot persuade the dictator that he is going down a dangerous path. England and France have done their best to encourage Hitler and have proven more than willing to sacrifice other countries to avoid war. Is Czechoslovakia next?

The Nazi Sphinx

SEPTEMBER 20, 1938. Hitler threatens Czechoslovakia in an effort to unite the German people of the Sudetenland with Germany. The Nazi leader hesitates, not knowing if Britain and France will go to war if he makes a grab for the Sudetenland. Americans think Britain and France will finally stand up to Hitler and he will back down.

Her 'Friends!'

SEPTEMBER 20, 1938. Britain and France turn their backs on Czechoslovakia in exchange for a false peace that won't last for long. Hitler masses troops on the Czech border and as is his custom puts out news reports protesting Czech troops attacking German troops along the border.

SEPTEMBER 22, 1938. Neville Chamberlain bows down to Hitler, sacrificing Czechoslovakia to Germany. France and Britain celebrate the phony peace thinking they have averted war and saved millions of lives. More lives will now be lost as Hitler continues to play Europe's democracies for fools. Like Austria, Czechoslovakia's fate is sealed.

SEPTEMBER 30, 1938. The execution of Lady Peace is delayed, and the leaders of France and Britain are hailed as heroes. Headlines of historic peace bring hope that there will never be war.

NOVEMBER 2, 1938. Mars makes a couple of sales. After all, he sells misery equally for anyone willing to buy. Hitler and Chamberlain both shake things up in their governments in an effort to maintain power. Hitler purges his army to help suppress plots to overthrow him as he leads his nation toward a destructive war. One of Hitler's purged generals was Ludwig Beck, who hoped to overthrow the dictator and took part in the failed Valkyrie assassination attempt on Hitler's life on July 20, 1944.

NOVEMBER 11, 1938. Armistice Day 1938, marking the end of the fighting in World War I, is celebrated. The armies of the world are on the march and are trampling on the memory of the millions of World War I dead. The drums of war grow louder and the fire of war burns brighter, as the world is on the march.

NOVEMBER 26, 1938.
France is threatened with a five-million-man strike on the home front from unhappy workers, which could lead to rioting. The United States speculates that the peace agreement at Munich with Hitler may not be worth celebrating and was instead additional nails in France's coffin. France signs a friendship pact with Nazi Germany, making themselves look weak in the eyes of America since their friend is busy butchering Jews at home and Czechoslovakians abroad.

Little Red Riding Hood

Happy New Year?

JANUARY 1, 1939. The year 1938 was a bad one for democracy and a bad year for the world. All signs are pointing to World War II. Bloody civil war continues in Spain, and Mussolini demands more French colonies while Hitler has managed to reduce France to a second rate world power through fear and capitulation. Small European countries band together in fear, trying to figure out how to preserve their independence with the land-grabbing Nazi menace still hungry.

JANUARY 10, 1939.
England's prime minister Neville Chamberlain heads to France and then to Rome to talk with Mussolini about his demands for French colonies. Appeasement doesn't seem to be working, as the dictators continue to make demands. Will France and England draw the line?

JANUARY 31, 1939. Hitler gives a speech in front of the German government on the sixth anniversary of his takeover of Germany. He continues to demand more room for Germans to live, making it plain that he will continue to threaten the outside world. Nothing is ever Hitler's fault, he is always defending himself against outside forces. Already persecuting Jewish citizens, he makes it clear that they will be annihilated in the next great war.

FEBRUARY 5, 1939.
Mussolini demands French colonial possessions, and Hitler will take more aggressive actions in 1939. He looks to make more land grabs using the same tactics as before. Hitler told his puppet government they stand with Mussolini, making it clear that they will aid and back up the fascist dictator.

FEBRUARY 12, 1939. The *Akron Beacon Journal* celebrates President Abraham Lincoln's birthday by encouraging Americans to embrace the spirit of Lincoln. In the face of tyranny and war, the United States needs Lincoln's tolerance, compassion, and faith in mankind as they see their government steering them into another great war. The United States, far from perfect, needs to preserve and improve its democracy by embracing the spirit of the great emancipator.

Don Roosevelt Quixote

—WEB. BROWN—

MARCH 2, 1939. Hermann Goering announces his Nazi air force is the greatest in the world and will continue to be the terror of the skies against Germany's enemies. The United States is busy spending $2 billion on armaments, including thousands of planes. Roosevelt's policy of increased armaments and support of Allies seems okay in theory but many question whether Britain would aid the United States or if they would turn their back on them to suit their own interests.

MARCH 3, 1939. In uncertain times and with growing threats to a just and peaceful world, a new pope is elected. Eugene Pacelli, who will be Pope Pius XII, will deal with an inhumane, anti-religion, and anti-freedom climate prevailing throughout Europe. Pius XII will have to show the world the way through the dark clouds of war, fear, intolerance, and oppression.

May He Show The Way To Peace

—WEB. BROWN—

MARCH 11, 1939. British prime minister Neville Chamberlain baffles the world by requesting a disarmament conference. No one in the world believes that the aggressor nations led by Hitler will disarm, nor will the democracies who are building up their armed forces to deal with the growing Nazi threat. Less than six months until the invasion of Poland, Chamberlain continues to show Hitler and the world he does not have what it takes to stop him.

He Needs A Shave, But ···

Revising The Classics

MARCH 15, 1939. The Ides of March was the day another conqueror of Europe, Julius Caesar, was assassinated. On this day, Hitler celebrates dividing up conquered Czechoslovakia into three different sections and the Nazi leader makes his first trip to Prague to gloat about his triumph.

His Pal

WHAT DO YOU SAY, OLD TOP— SHALL WE LET BYGONES BE BYGONES?

—WEB.BROWN—

MARCH 21, 1939.
America watches and finds it humorous that Great Britain, a country that has ignored and scorned Russia for 20 years, including snubbing Russia recently at Munich, now reaches out to them. Britain and France falsely thought at Munich they could stop Hitler with no help from Russia. Now that Hitler has violated the Munich agreement, the uneasy democracies of Britain and France are ready to make Russia their new pal.

MARCH 24, 1939.
Memelland, taken from Germany and given to Lithuania following World War I, is demanded by and given to Hitler by the Lithuanians. "Heil liar," newspapers like the *Beacon Journal* read as Hitler's appetite for more land keeps gobbling up more territory. The world is starting to realize that there is no bargaining with Hitler. The time to talk is coming closer to an end. War is approaching.

Saying It With Brickbats

WHAT, AGAIN?!

—WEB.BROWN—

MARCH 31, 1939. The Nazis begin threatening Poland with the same type of propaganda used in the Czechoslovakian crisis. Neville Chamberlain of Britain, who a few weeks ago was so delusional he was suggesting a disarmament conference to avert a future war, now says that Britain will fight if Poland is invaded. Damocles only had one sword hanging over his head; the world has five in the tumultuous year of 1939.

Damocles Was A Piker

Careful, Sam --- It's Loaded!

APRIL 7, 1939. Congress debates neutrality law revisions as war seems near in Europe. The United States was neutral in 1917 but was still dragged into that war by propaganda, unrestricted submarine warfare, and the actions of Woodrow Wilson. Many Americans feel neutrality legislation can't keep them out of a war and that President Roosevelt plans to aid the democracies and push the United States into a war.

33

On The Powder Keg

APRIL 11, 1939. The powder keg won't explode yet to ignite the Second World War. The two dictators, Hitler and Mussolini, have gotten away with a lot of land grabs without having to fight. This has only encouraged them to demand more land. Mussolini signs a nonaggression pact with Greece, which should be seen as a worthless promise. Britain maneuvers ships to block Mussolini from further action in the Adriatic Sea.

APRIL 14, 1939. Mussolini and Hitler are embarking on the path of Napoleon Bonaparte. France has no desire to see a non-Frenchman carry out the conquering of Europe, and Britain also realizes her security and possessions are threatened. More than willing to break treaties themselves and give away Austria and Czechoslovakia, France and Britain change their tune when it's going to affect them. France and Britain together let the two dictators know war is likely if they make any more land grabs.

Read The Fine Print, Too, Boys

34

APRIL 16, 1939. President Roosevelt makes an appeal for a long-term peace pledge in Europe, which should only be laughed at in Germany and encourage Hitler. Hitler has no plans for peace, so asking him is idiotic. President Roosevelt suggests a 10-year nonaggression pledge. A nonaggression pledge from a man who will break that pledge anytime he feels like it.

No Game For Us

The Birthday Cake

APRIL 20, 1939. Mussolini and Hitler celebrate Hitler's birthday as Mussolini rejects President Roosevelt's request for a nonaggression pact by saying that peace is the policy of the Axis. Hitler will give his response to Roosevelt in a week in front of his puppet government. Roosevelt's request of a nonaggression pact followed by a disarmament conference seems incredibly naïve.

35

They Want A Little Help

WE'LL PROTECT YOUR INDEPENDENCE—

IF YOU WILL PROTECT OURS!

APRIL 22, 1939. England, France, and Russia talk of protecting each other's independence as fear of Hitler grows. Newspapers point out that there is no shame of being afraid; the United States is over 4,000 miles from the battle zone and is so scared of what is to come that they are rapidly building up their armed forces. Hitler, a bully, eyes Eastern European countries with populations less than two million. They are helpless against the better equipped 85 million people of Germany.

APRIL 23, 1939. The centuries-old children's tale "Babes in the Woods" is reworked for the tumultuous year of 1939. Instead of children dying in the woods and being covered with leaves by birds, peace and civilization die with gas masks on while being covered in leaves by planes—or are those bombs?

Babes In The Woods --- 1939 Style

MAY 21, 1939. The United States gets ready for the first ever visit to America by a sitting British monarch. King George VI and Queen Elizabeth will visit the United States in June of 1939 and Americans are skeptical. The British monarch's break from tradition by visiting the United States on the eve of World War II is interpreted by many as an effort to draw America into the war on the side of the English, just like in 1917.

JUNE 8, 1939. The spirit of King George III looks on as King George VI and Queen Elizabeth are warmly welcomed in America. Millions of Americans will venture out to see the king and queen, the first British monarchs to visit the United States, on their four-day trip. Many Americans know Prime Minister Chamberlain sent the king and queen to America on a mission to draw support as war nears.

37

Overlooking The Parent Porcupine

POLAND

ACH – LOOK BEHIND THE TREE, ADOLF!

GERMAN PEOPLE

SH-H-H – HE'S AS GOOD AS IN THE BAG NOW!

DANZIG

HITLER

JUNE 22, 1939. Hitler and his propaganda minister Joseph Goebbels continue to demand the Danzig region from Poland. Britain is in talks with Russia on a pact which would stop Hitler from invading Poland. Hitler knows Poland, Britain, and France will fight him if he invades Poland and he thinks he can take them. Talks with Russia are not going well for Britain, and Hitler waits for his opportunity.

JUNE 24, 1939. Prime Minister Neville Chamberlain gives a fighting speech that is cheered in London after years of appeasement. In the speech, Chamberlain warns Germany and Japan of its willingness to stand up to any aggressors with the best navy in the world and an air force that cannot be matched by any country. Japan lifts a blockade of British ships in Swatow, China, as tensions continue to rise.

The Sun Never Sets

JAPANESE CRISIS

JOHN BULL

CHINA

JUNE 28, 1939. Mars spins the globe on the 25th anniversary of Archduke Ferdinand's assassination in Sarajevo, which sparked World War I. The assassination, known as the shot heard around the world, left millions dead. Everyone knows the next war will be far more destructive and the spark that will set it off could come from anywhere.

AUGUST 18, 1939. Poland lets Hitler know they plan to fight rather than hand over Danzig. Newspaper writer William Philip Simms put the odds at three to one in favor of peace after talking to many European leaders.

Left At The Post

AUGUST 22, 1939. Germany makes a nonaggression pact with Russia, which will allow them to invade Poland without having to fight a two-front war. Hitler, who wrote about conquering and wiping out Russia in *Mein Kampf,* convinced Stalin to make this agreement. This pact is devastating to Russia, to the world, and of course to Poland, who is in immediate danger.

WORLD DIPLOMACY SWEEPSTAKES PRIZE RUSSIAN AID

AUGUST 23, 1939. Rumors in Europe run wild after Russia and Germany sign a nonaggression pact. Britain and France let Hitler and the world know there will be no more appeasement. If Hitler moves on Poland, there will be war. The world waits as Europe and Poland's fates are in the gravedigger's hands.

The Grave Digger

AUGUST 29, 1939. Hitler decides whether it's peace or war. Poland is doomed, and most observers agree that Poland will be devastated in the coming conflict before it's over. The *Beacon Journal* reports that it's a game of heads you lose, tails you lose if you're Poland.

AUGUST 31, 1939. On the eve of World War II, all telegraphic and phone communications from Europe to the United States go silent. Britain mobilizes its entire navy and calls up its army and air reserves. Hitler hints at Russian aid as he continues to pressure Poland. Mars wins; the light is going out.

41

Three

WAR ERUPTS
SEPTEMBER 1, 1931–DECEMBER 6, 1941

SEPTEMBER 5, 1939.
Hitler's plan of conquest
laid out in *Mein
Kampf* is in motion.

SEPTEMBER 19, 1939. Poland hopes for a miracle as Nazi troops are only 20 miles from the capital of Warsaw. Fighting the Germans is bad enough for Poland, who is fighting bravely. It has become apparent that Hitler's nonaggression pact with Russia included giving them part of Poland. Stalin, a greedy and ruthless dictator himself, took the bait and Poland is caught in a vise fighting both countries.

In The Jaws Of A Vise

The Best Method

SEPTEMBER 22, 1939. President Roosevelt outlines American neutrality policies as war starts in Europe. The cash-and-carry policy is enacted, and Americans cannot travel on ships of belligerent nations. American merchant ships may not enter war zones either. Americans look to avoid the mistakes made between 1914 and 1917 that drew them into World War I.

Trophy Of The Hunt

SEPTEMBER 23, 1939. Poland is on the verge of defeat and Germany and Russia have already begun to divide the spoils. After stabbing Poland in the back, many wonder what's next from Russia. Hitler and Stalin are expected to divide the Baltic and Balkan countries next. But how long will their love affair last?

SEPTEMBER 24, 1939. Stalin, the Hitler of Russia, enjoys some reading as he eyes more land grabs in Eastern Europe. Romania's leader was recently assassinated by a pro-Nazi group. After receiving and taking land for herself at the end of World War I, Romania has a lot of land Russia and Germany would like for themselves.

The Pupil

WHY DIDN'T I HEAR ABOUT THIS FELLOW'S METHODS BEFORE?

44

NOVEMBER 11, 1939. Words from Abraham Lincoln's Gettysburg Address are referenced on Armistice Day 1939. The Tomb of the Unknown Soldier was erected in 1921 after World War I. Americans and World War I veterans are determined not to get drawn back into another European war. Nobody wants another 1917.

FEBRUARY 14, 1940. Mars is there to greet Sumner Welles wherever he goes in Europe on a mission of peace and disarmament. He will visit Germany, Italy, France, and England. Some critics say FDR is going to use the war as an excuse to run for a third term and claim if he gets it he will see it as a mandate to get more involved in European affairs.

Waiting For Orders

MARCH 19, 1940. Hitler and Mussolini have a secret meeting on a train at Brenner Pass. What they talk about no one knows. One thing most observers note, the meeting was not likely a good sign for the Allies. Mars won't likely be turning this train toward peace, as Hitler will only accept a peace agreeable to him. Most likely, Mars will be taking the path of intensive warfare as the weather breaks this spring for a new offensive.

APRIL 6, 1940. On the 23rd anniversary of the United States entering World War I, America lets Europe know that they wish to have no part of the second chapter. Peace rallies will be held throughout the country including one sponsored by Akron's Keep out of Foreign Wars Committee. The *Akron Beacon Journal* headline reads, "U.S. cured of war fever on anniversary of 1917."

APRIL 14, 1940. Germany invades Norway and Denmark, and many fear that Belgium, the Netherlands, and the Balkan countries will be next. Most Americans are determined to stay neutral and object to newspapers, politicians, and other groups giving France and Britain the impression that the United States will come to their aid if they are on the verge of defeat.

Pinocchio

Happy Birthday?

APRIL 20, 1940. On his birthday, the Nazi leader gets his gift of countless war dead as the results of his actions. The Allies struggle to remove the Nazis from Norway and Churchill announces a summer offensive to do just that. The fact that the Allies could not repulse Hitler in Norway may be a bad sign for other small countries hoping the Allies can help them.

Blueprint Yesterday, In Execution Today

MAY 10, 1940. Hitler invades Holland, Belgium, and Luxembourg, and the German army's blitzkrieg tactics are achieving quick success.

MAY 11, 1940. Hitler invades Luxembourg, Belgium, and Holland to preserve their neutrality. The dictator always makes up lies to justify each invasion or aggressive action. Bombings of defenseless cities and the killing of civilians that are in the path of war are part of what the neutral countries will experience during the Nazi blitzkrieg.

To Preserve Their Neutrality

MAY 14, 1940. Ex-Kaiser Wilhelm can now watch Nazi planes go about their work from his castle at Doorn in the Netherlands. Wilhelm, who sent his invading German army through neutral Belgium during World War I, had success at first too. The people at home united behind him in the early years of the war. At exile in the Netherlands, Wilhelm serves as a reminder to Hitler of what may become of him after his luck runs out.

MAY 25, 1940. During World War I, as the dead were buried, beautiful red poppies began to grow between the white crosses, prompting Canadian soldier John McCrae to write the popular poem "In Flanders Field." On Buddy Poppy Day 1940, American veterans of 1917–1918 reflect on the horror of war as the poppies blow once again.

Watch That First Step!

UNITED, THE ITALIAN NATION GOES FORWARD TO MEET ITS DESTINY!

ITALIAN PEOPLE

WILL FOR PEACE

DUCE

DECLARATION OF WAR

WEB. BROWN

JUNE 4, 1940. The Germans are driving on Paris and Mussolini, who can't hope to beat anybody who can fight back, considers jumping in the fight as it nears its conclusion. While Hitler's troops march all the way to Paris, the Italians manage to wrestle away around 100 yards from the French.

JULY 20, 1940. England rejects Hitler's offer of peace. The Nazi dictator has promised destruction if Britain does not accept. Outnumbered and outgunned, Britain hopes the English Channel, their superior navy, and fighting spirit can repel Nazi attacks and prevent an invasion. A gamble, for sure, but what alternative do they have? No one can blame Britain for not accepting the kind of peace Hitler offers.

A Voice From The Graveyard

MY POLICY HAS BEEN FRIENDSHIP!

OFFER OF PEACE TO ENGLAND

HITLER

HOLLAND   POLAND   NORWAY

FRANCE   DENMARK

CZECHOSLOVAKIA   AUSTRIA   LUXEMBOURG

WEB BROWN

JULY 27, 1940. The British endure Nazi bombing raids and furiously defend themselves in the air and at sea. The Battle of Britain has begun. The British will use the advantage of their advancements in radar to track and battle incoming enemy planes.

Not Conquered Yet!

What Would They Think Of It?

AUGUST 23, 1940. The ghosts of George Washington and Thomas Jefferson read the headline of a possible alliance with their former foe. George Washington warned in his farewell presidential address to not get involved in the constant fighting in Europe and to instead use America's distance across the Atlantic to keep out of European wars. Many Americans reference Washington's address as America marched toward war in both World War I and World War II.

Lightning Rod

AUGUST 25, 1940. The Battle of Britain rages as the Nazis launch a blitzkrieg from the sky throughout the summer of 1940 against the British Royal Air Force. In the United States, Congress debates the Burke Wadsworth conscription bill introduced in June 1940, as America became concerned about the British being quickly defeated. Opponents of the conscription bill point out that Britain has been successfully defending themselves against the Nazi raiders.

AUGUST 27, 1940. Hitler has brought the horrors of bombings by airplanes to many European cities. Helsinki, Paris, London, Warsaw, and Brussels to name a few. The Royal Air Force recently has brought the same horrors to the people of Berlin. Hitler was winning the Battle of Britain until he lost his temper after the bombing of Berlin and began focusing on bombing London instead of wiping out the RAF.

A Chapter Adolf Didn't Write

AUGUST 30, 1940. The Senate votes 58 to 31 to start conscription while at peace for the first time in United States history. Americans now fear that the Army will not be built up for defense and peace, but for war. The conscription bill is passed out of fear of the Germans but it will allow President Roosevelt to be tougher on other countries, like Japan.

The Hand That Did The Signing

Birthday

SEPTEMBER 1, 1940. World War II turns a year old. Hitler and the world should keep in mind that it's not the first year of war that is the toughest but the last. Europe has been drenched in blood that has spilled over into Africa. China and Japan are fighting a separate war, but many wonder if their war will join its larger counterpart in Europe to create bloodshed from Gibraltar to Tokyo.

Is This A No-Limit Game?

SEPTEMBER 28, 1940. Mars and President Roosevelt play a game of poker as America now proposes sending flying fortress bombers over to Britain. Americans see the increased aid of Great Britain as a ticket into the war they don't want. The *Beacon Journal* campaigned all summer against the conscription bill as they believe it will lead to more aggressive actions that will get America in the war.

Three Would-Be Napoleons

SEPTEMBER 29, 1940. The Germans, Italians, and Japanese make a 10-year military and economic pact. The agreement is made out of fear of increased US involvement in Europe and embargoes against Japanese aggression. Hitler and Japan do not understand that the United States does not scare easily. Something like this just makes Americans mad. Everyone knows Hitler despises Japan, so their pact is a farce from the start.

54

OCTOBER 5, 1940. Hitler and Mussolini meet, the Germans' initial success last spring and early summer has stalled, and the Axis is struggling. Mussolini always struggles, but Hitler is also having trouble with the British. Despite what the Axis press says, the meeting between Mussolini and Hitler reeks of desperation. They need a victory, and these two love soft targets.

OCTOBER 16, 1940. Uncle Sam does some recruiting, and America's young men register for the draft. The wheels of war are in motion, and as President Roosevelt builds up his army he will begin more aggressive actions in both the Atlantic and the Pacific. The draft is supposed to be for defense, but as President Roosevelt has a bigger army to back him up, he will begin to talk and act tougher.

What's A Little Treachery Between Friends?

—WEB.BROWN.

OCTOBER 23, 1940. Word is out that Hitler has offered Pierre Laval of France an easy peace if France declares war on Great Britain. France is unlikely to trust Hitler and fight their former ally. Once again, Hitler's actions reek of desperation. Unable to invade and conquer Britain, Hitler looks for leverage.

On The March

OCTOBER 30, 1940. The World War I fishbowl used for drawing for the draft of the first Great War is brought out for the peacetime draft of World War II. It takes over 17 hours of drawing numbers to get 17 million men numbered for conscription. The draft is started due to the German menace, but it will be Japan that gets America in the war.

NOVEMBER 12, 1940.
Americans, who always love an underdog, are thrilled to hear reports that the Greeks are chasing Mussolini's army back into Albania. A whole Italian division is reported to be annihilated as the Italians retreat. Everyone remembers Russia losing battle after battle to the brave forces of Finland in 1940 only to see them eventually give in. The same is still expected in Greece, especially if Hitler intervenes.

And It Looked Like A Soft Touch

Meeting Unexpected Resistance

NOVEMBER 17, 1940. Russia makes a deal with its Axis partners for its own sphere once the war is over. It seems likely Hitler was growing concerned that the British may persuade Stalin to ally himself with them as Russia might be growing concerned about a German invasion. Hitler is not having success at knocking out the British and Mussolini is doing even worse in Greece. He cannot afford to lose Stalin yet.

Thankful, Most Of All, For Freedom

NOVEMBER 21, 1940.
Thanksgiving is celebrated in
1940. While many countries
of the world have lost their
freedom, the United States is
thankful to still have theirs.
Many lament the unprecedented
militarization of America in a
time of peace with conscription
having begun. Americans believe
conscription was necessary for
national defense, but they do
not realize that the defense of
America will take place far from
home in the coming years.

Sinking Fast

NOVEMBER 30, 1940. Greece,
with help from Great Britain,
continues to have success against
Mussolini's Italian forces. The
Italian army so far has suffered
humiliating and costly defeats.
No aid has come from Hitler,
and the British Navy and Air
Force have wreaked havoc
on Italian supply lines while
Greece has pushed the enemy
out of their country and are
attacking inside Albania.

DECEMBER 8, 1940. American employment is at record levels of 46 million, which had not been seen since the 47 million days of 1929. Defense activity and war production drops unemployment by one million men in a year with a prediction of six million more jobs in the coming year. With greater paychecks and prosperity, Americans celebrate the end of the Great Depression, though many despise the cause.

DECEMBER 11, 1940. Hitler shows no signs of slowing down his war of conquest but speaks cautiously to his people as they have concerns about his lack of success as the sun sets on 1940. Blatantly lying to his people in one sentence and telling the truth the next, Hitler's recent speech to his people indicates morale is low in Germany and the war is taking its toll.

Dynamiting The Sea Wall

DECEMBER 19, 1940. Fresh off reelection after defeating Wendell Willkie in the presidential race of 1940, President Roosevelt begins to target the neutrality act in an effort to aid Britain. This is the beginning of President Roosevelt's lend lease program. President Roosevelt has vowed that American soldiers won't have to fight on foreign soil. Will he go back on those words?

Not Asking Much

DECEMBER 21, 1940. Benito Mussolini turns to Santa Claus for a little help; after all, it's the season for giving. The Italian army is surrendering in large numbers in Greece, Albania, and Africa. Many speculate they don't want to fight and Mussolini desperately needs a victory to avoid being overthrown at home.

60

DECEMBER 27, 1940. America follows sensational reports of German troop trains moving into Rumania. 300,000 German troops joining the 100,000 already stationed there. Hitler doesn't need that many soldiers to police Rumania nor to fight Turkey or Greece. Analysts speculate that a major battle between Russia and Germany may be coming, which may help Britain win the war.

JANUARY 7, 1941. The *Beacon Journal* editorial titled "We're in the War" outlines President Roosevelt's undeclared war with increasing aid to Britain and other Allies. Americans do not want a repeat of World War I, but President Roosevelt is ignoring and dismantling the neutrality acts aggressively in the early days after his reelection.

Time Bomb

WHAT SHALL WE DO WITH IT, ADOLF?

MUSSOLINI

ROOSEVELT'S SPEECH

—WEB.BROWN—

JANUARY 8, 1941. In President Roosevelt's recent speech he does something Hitler and Mussolini are not used to; he talks tough about destroying the totalitarian countries. Roosevelt, time and again, insists that America increase and keep increasing its aid to Britain and others. That aid will be used to attack the Axis, and Mussolini and Hitler for the first time will wonder what to do with a nation actively seeking their destruction without officially being in the war.

JANUARY 18, 1941. Secretary of the Navy Frank Knox, a newspaperman himself, proposes a censorship plan to gag the press while the nation is at peace. The *Akron Beacon Journal* points out that there are only two reasons to censor the press: war or dictatorship. Mars approves, but newspapers across the country insist on reporting the news in times of peace and not hiding the facts that may get them involved in a war.

The Secretary Forgets That The Nation Is At Peace

SAY, THAT'S GREAT; MOST DEMOCRACIES WAIT UNTIL THEY ARE AT WAR BEFORE THEY GAG THE PRESS!

MARS

KNOX

CENSORSHIP PLAN

—WEB.BROWN—

JANUARY 19, 1941. President Roosevelt is sworn in for an unprecedented third term as president of the United States. The historic depression of the 1930s propelled him to office in 1933 and a historic war prompted him to run for and win a third term. The depression is ending as the war clouds move in to bring a greater threat to the United States.

And We Thought It Was Dark In 1933!

1933 — DEPRESSION — WAR HYSTERIA — 1941

Ending A Beautiful Dream

DREAM OF EMPIRE — GREEK VICTORIES — AFRICAN ROUT — MUSSOLINI

JANUARY 26, 1941. Mussolini's dream of an empire is about to burst. Italian forces are being routed in Africa as the Greek Army continues to claim more victories. Mussolini entered World War II as he saw the Allies were collapsing under the German onslaught of 1940. Now that he has faced numerous humiliating defeats, many hope he won't be in power much longer.

The Referee Intervenes

YOU TAKE A DIVE IN THE NEXT ROUND! GET ME?

GREECE

HITLER

MUSSOLINI

—WEB. BROWN

FEBRUARY 20, 1941. The world wonders when Hitler might intervene and stop the beating his pal Mussolini was taking for months at the hands of Greece. Reports of German planes flying over Athens and a threatened German invasion of Greece through Bulgaria has everyone convinced that Germany has finally decided to save their Axis partner.

APRIL 6, 1941. On the 24th anniversary of the United States entering World War I, America sees itself heading in the same direction. Mars is there once again as the last book to complete the set is about to be written. It is true, the United States will not make it out of 1941 without entering the war they all hoped to avoid.

One More Book Will Complete The Set

WAR

DIPLOMATIC EXCHANGES — DIPLOMATIC EXCHANGES

ARMED NEUTRALITY — ALL-OUT AID

PREPAREDNESS — AID SHORT OF WAR

FREEDOM OF THE SEAS — NATIONAL DEFENSE

NEUTRALITY

1917 — 1941

MARS

HISTORY

INK

—WEB. BROWN

APRIL 10, 1941. The British announce their war budget of $20 billion for the coming year in their commitment to see this war through. Some income brackets will pay 50 percent of their income, while the more prosperous classes will pay up to 97.5% of their income to fund this massive war effort. John Bull fights on, and their citizens continue to sacrifice to avoid becoming the next Nazi victim.

Undaunted

But That's All He Had

HOW SAD! HE HAD MY SYMPATHY!

APRIL 11, 1941. The day after signing a friendship pact with Russia, Yugoslavia is crushed by the Nazis. The prospects of a conflict between Russia and Germany grow. Russia says they want peace and have done everything they can to promote peace. Their actions from Poland to Finland say otherwise, and now they may have to battle the other supposed peace lover, Hitler.

Modern Moses

APRIL 12, 1941. President Roosevelt allows American ships to enter the Red Sea, which is safe for now but threatened by the intensifying warfare nearby. Americans see this as FDR more actively participating in the war and not as an act of defense like he always says. To some, the president is increasingly engaging in naval warfare.

APRIL 16, 1941. Hitler and the Germans begin to turn the tide in Greece and Africa. The British are reported to be evacuating troops, and it seems it won't be long before Greece has to surrender. Mussolini is likely to take Albania back and the British now have a growing Axis threat in the Mediterranean Sea and Africa.

Modern Olympic Games

APRIL 20, 1941. Greek premier Alexander Korizis commits suicide as the Axis and the grim reaper have their day in the Balkans. The killing in World War II had not been as great as expected at first, but reports of 50,000 dead in the fighting in Greece. Not to mention that the bloodletting in Yugoslavia provides a bumper crop of lives this spring.

Balkan Spring Scene

Pre-War Crescendo

APRIL 25, 1941. Mars leads a band of Americans promoting President Roosevelt's policies designed to get the United States involved in World War II. The call is for the convoying of ships which President Roosevelt himself said wouldn't happen when he ask approval for his Lend Lease program. Convoys mean war, and nobody likes convoys like Mars!

67

The Landslide Has Started

MAY 6, 1941. Wendell Willkie is one of many Americans that think naval patrols are not enough and that the United States should begin convoying to protect merchant ships. The landslide toward war has started, and the momentum cannot be stopped. 85 percent of Americans favor aiding Britain, and 85 percent of Americans favor America staying out of the war. You can't have it both ways.

Government In Russia Undergoes A Great Change

MAY 8, 1941. Stalin takes over the title of premier of Russia from Vyacheslav Molotov, which may signal a break with Nazi Germany. Russia, a country of 175 million, is controlled by the Communist dictator Joseph Stalin and his Communist Party, which is only made up of two to three million members. Stalin has been firmly in charge since Vladimir Lenin's death in 1924.

JUNE 5, 1941. The death of Kaiser Wilhelm, Germany's leader during World War I, reminds Hitler that his time is coming, too. Hitler will join other dictators bent on conquest—the likes of Napoleon and Caesar. Wilhelm will be remembered for militarism, sorrow, hunger, poverty, and bitter disillusionment.

Cheerful Thought

Still Hungry?

JUNE 17, 1941. German troops continue to mass on the Russian border, and many speculate that Russia is about to be invaded. Britain, however, cautions that it may be a smokescreen and the Nazis are trying to divert attention away from the real goal, the long awaited invasion of England. After observing Russia's failures in Finland, Hitler might think he can easily seize the vast resources of Russia.

End Of Detour

JUNE 24, 1941. Hitler attacks Russia, just like he said he would in *Mein Kampf.* Germany's attack on Russia convinces the United States that Hitler will invade anybody and is a danger to America. It should be pointed out he abandoned invading Britain because he couldn't do it and instead went after the less prepared and battle-tested Russian army.

A Young American Comes Of Age

JULY 2, 1941. Men who have turned 21 since the draft was first instituted in October 1940 are required to register for the draft at the start of July 1941. The *Beacon Journal* put it best: "Old men make the mistakes and young men do the fighting."

JULY 6, 1941. Death overshadows the battlefields of Russia. Just like when they fought Napoleon in 1812, Russia is willing to destroy its crops and land rather than leave it for the invading Germany army. The bloody fighting will continue, but as supplies get low death will continue to take its toll on both sides.

Overshadowing The Battle In Russia

Keeping Busy, Adolph?

AUGUST 5, 1941. Mars gives Hitler another ball to juggle. Russia has fought well enough for six weeks. A quick victory and Moscow are nowhere in sight for the German army. The British continue to bomb Germany and the Nazis face sporadic revolts in conquered countries. The Nazis are not beat, but the tide of the war seems to be turning.

71

AUGUST 21, 1941. Fresh off a historic secret meeting at sea with Winston Churchill, President Roosevelt says that America needs to help crush Hitler or face invasion. Hitler can't even make it across the English Channel to invade England, so FDR is exaggerating the Nazi threat to get support for his increased involvement in the war. Stalin, America's future cold war nemesis, gets US aid, as America will supply anyone fighting the Axis.

AUGUST 24, 1941. Army morale is low as the majority of the men serving were originally drafted or called to service were told they would serve one year. In August 1941, Congress extended their length of service from one year to two and a half years. They have had to train with inadequate weapons and outdated training with incompetent officers. Meanwhile, those who are not serving are making money in the booming war economy.

September 6, 1941. The United States destroyer *Greer* is fired on by a German sub, and it returns fire during the incident. Neither sub nor destroyer are hit. President Roosevelt makes a big deal out of the incident and calls for the sub to be sunk. A congressional investigation later found that the *Greer* wasn't minding its own business like the president said. It was actively tracking the sub and communicating with a British plane that was dropping depth charges on it when the incident occurred.

September 7, 1941. American planes are starting to turn out at a higher rate, and many are being sent to Britain to use against the Axis. In January 1941, a total of 1,036 planes were produced. Production jumped only to 1,460 by July but bounded to 1,854 in August. That monthly rate would produce 20,000 planes a year, far below President Roosevelt's goal of 50,000.

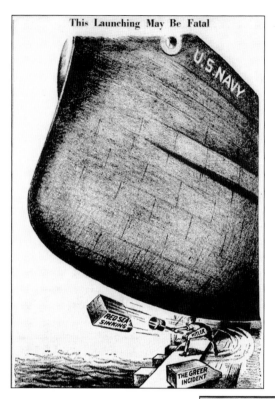

This Launching May Be Fatal

SEPTEMBER 10, 1941. An incident in the Red Sea and with the destroyer *Greer* has President Roosevelt fired up. Hitler may be faced with an increasing undeclared naval war that may eventually lead to all-out war with the United States. The only irony is that Hitler does not want America in the war and is trying not to sink American ships. Easier said than done.

All Ears

SEPTEMBER 11, 1941. The world waits to hear President Roosevelt's fireside chat after several recent incidents between American ships and German subs and one in the Red Sea with a German plane. It is expected that President Roosevelt will announce a new policy that will bring the United States closer to a shooting war in the Atlantic.

SEPTEMBER 12, 1941. President Roosevelt gives his famous shoot-on-sight order, which includes his reference to the Germans as the rattlesnakes of the Atlantic. Whenever the US Navy encounters an Axis rattlesnake they are ordered to shoot on sight. As the *Beacon Journal* editorial team saw it, Americans have been in the war since Lend Lease was passed and it is a waste of time to talk about keeping out.

Rattlesnake Hunter

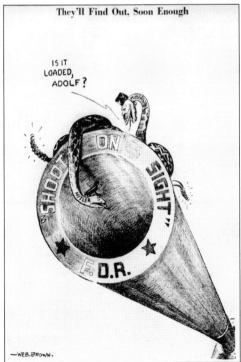

They'll Find Out, Soon Enough

SEPTEMBER 13, 1941. Now that the United States has vowed to shoot enemy ships on sight, it will have to back up that tough talk. The United States is not officially at war. President Roosevelt is simply calling his actions a defensive measure. Hitler doesn't want the United States to enter a war he is already struggling to win. Despite tough talk, the Axis isn't looking for trouble.

Maybe It's Something He Ate

SEPTEMBER 30, 1941. Hitler has had too much to eat, and things aren't going well in Russia. Even Yugoslavia has been up against three German divisions and still won't be quiet. They are living up to the old Serbian proverb, "a grave ever, a slave never." The tide is turning against Hitler, and the United States is not even officially in the war—yet.

Oh Yeah?

" I CAN SAY TODAY THAT THIS OPPONENT HAS ALREADY BEEN BEATEN ---- HITLER

OCTOBER 4, 1941. "Hitler is a liar. There is no doubt about that." The *Akron Beacon Journal* is still surprised to see him claim victory for his army when they are still facing massive resistance throughout Russia. Hitler's enemies see this as a sign that he is losing.

OCTOBER 18, 1941. A German U-boat hits the *USS Kearny* in American waters 250 miles from Iceland, which should give Congress more reason to speed the repeal of the Neutrality Act. Surprisingly, the United States reaction to the Kearny incident doesn't strike its usual tone. Prince Konye has lost power in Japan to the militaristic Hideki Tojo, and for the first time the United States seems to think trouble in the Pacific is brewing.

You're Likely To Get Hurt, Adolf

Not As Serviceable As It Looked

OCTOBER 22, 1941. The Neutrality Act has been constantly under attack since World War II started. Designed to keep America out of World War II, it failed to do its job. Cash and Carry was the first dagger, then Lend Lease, and later came convoys that FDR had promised not to use in the spring of 1941. Now FDR is asking for armed merchant ships, and it won't be long before the neutrality act is dead.

NOVEMBER 11, 1941. The 23rd anniversary of the end of World War I, or Armistice Day, is celebrated. The *Akron Beacon Journal* received a call to ask if Armistice Day would continue to be celebrated on November 11th in the future or if there would be a different Armistice Day after World War II. After the Korean War, President Eisenhower changed Armistice Day to Veterans Day as America gave up on celebrating peace.

NOVEMBER 16, 1941.
US merchant marines will now be voyaging everywhere and delivering supplies to defeat the Axis, and Hitler in particular. The Germans have a lot to fear of increased US involvement. Lend Lease aid to both Britain and Russia has helped keep both countries from being knocked out of the war. In the coming years, that same aid, will help win the war.

DECEMBER 2, 1941. The Germans are in retreat in Russia and in Africa. Hitler continues to struggle to put away the British and the Russians. Five days until Pearl Harbor, things are about to get worse for the man hell-bent on world conquest. Hitler's armies are stalled, just like the German forces in World War I. The United States entry into the war will help defeat Germany once again.

Four

WAKING THE GIANT
DECEMBER 7, 1941–APRIL 28, 1944

DECEMBER 13, 1941. Following the Japanese attack of Pearl Harbor on December 7, 1941, Congress quickly declares war on the Axis. Americans pledge to see it through to total victory. The Russians repel Hitler's forces, who are now forced to call off their offensive for the winter. Word is out that the Germans have hinted they would be willing to make a peace agreement with Russia. Distrustful after making a peace agreement with Germany in 1939, the Russians refuse and recommend annihilation of the Nazis as a prelude to peace.

December 17, 1941. Hitler is ordered to take a rest cure from exhaustion at his retreat in Berchtesgaden while German soldiers are retreating from Moscow. The year 1941 has not gone well for Hitler. He lost the Battle of Britain; chose to invade Russia, where he is now in retreat; and faced increasing hostility from the United States, which culminated with a declaration of war this month.

December 23, 1941. "If 1941 was the crucial year—and we believe Hitler was right when he so described it—then the would-be world conqueror has missed his chance and is headed for certain defeat," the *Akron Beacon Journal* opines. Hitler is eating his words, as many of the things he has said have not come true.

Graduation Day

JUNE 7, 1942. The class of 1942, the first spring graduating class of the war, get their diplomas. Prime fighting and draft age, the majority of these men will be picking up a rifle with a bayonet to fight. The *Akron Beacon Journal* said it best: "The young men need to win the war caused by the mistakes of the older generation."

Something To Cheer About

THAT'S MORE LIKE IT!

CORAL SEA VICTORY
MIDWAY
TREATIES
SECOND FRONT PLANNED

JUNE 13, 1942. Admiral Yamamoto, the man who planned the Pearl Harbor attack, was not confident in Japan ultimately winning the war. In the spring of 1942, Japan's naval advance toward Australia is halted at the Battle of the Coral Sea and is followed by the Japanese navy being routed at the Battle of Midway. Six months after Pearl Harbor, the Japanese Navy is headed back toward Japan.

JULY 31, 1942. The Battle of Stalingrad, one of the bloodiest battles of World War II, is approaching. Germans are having success on the battlefields of Russia in the summer of 1942, and Stalin orders his troops to stand their ground. In fact, the Russian army sets up machine guns and tells their troops that if they retreat they will be shot. Russian soldiers have to fight and win or fight and die.

With His Back To The Wall

'NOT ONE STEP BACK!'
—STALIN

Zero Hour For A Second Front

RUSSIA'S RESISTANCE

AUGUST 9, 1942. Russian resistance is running out as Hitler drives on the Caucasus oil fields. The *Akron Beacon Journal* makes the case for a second front to help the Russians. Experts think that if Hitler grabs the Caucasus oil field he can then easily conquer the oil fields of the Middle East.

Moses Of 1942

HOPE OF VICTORY

AUGUST 11, 1942. The countries of the world are turning to Uncle Sam for aid and leadership during the Second World War. America will supply a significant portion of the weapons and other aid needed for victory to many of these countries. These countries, which have fought valiantly against the Axis Powers, will need our fresh troops to enter the battlefields to open up a second front and relieve their exhausted armies in order to win the war.

Avenue Of Triumph

SEPTEMBER 18, 1942. Bloody fighting takes place on the streets of Stalingrad and the cost on both sides is extraordinary. It was assumed at the time that the Russian city was on the verge of falling to the Nazis. In fact, the Nazis took over most of the city but once again were unprepared for winter and were driven out of the city by spring.

OCTOBER 9, 1942. Hitler will answer for his crimes across Europe once the war is over. President Roosevelt announces that when the war is over the United Nations will demand the surrender of all war criminals. "The ringleaders responsible for organized murder of thousands of innocent persons," he says, will be brought to justice.

OCTOBER 13, 1942. Early in the war, Hitler brought the horrors of aerial warfare to cities throughout Europe even bombing defenseless cities with no remorse. The Germans tried to bomb the British into submission in the Battle of Britain. In the coming years, Germany will be on the receiving end of relentless and horrific bombing.

Between The Devil And The Deep Blue Sea

—WEB.BROWN

NOVEMBER 20, 1942. General Rommel's forces have been driven into Tunisia, where the American, British, and free French have the Axis trapped against the Mediterranean Sea. In the next several months, close to 300,000 Axis troops will be captured as they are forced out of Africa—another major defeat for Hitler's forces. The Italian people are nervous and they ought to be, for the Allies are on their doorstep.

NOVEMBER 21, 1942. Things are not going well in Africa, and the Russians are in the process of launching a winter offensive to dislodge the Germans from Stalingrad. Hitler's forces will have a second winter of losses in Russia and will likely never hold as much Russian territory again due to those losses. Word is the Italians want peace and the Germans may have to occupy Italy to keep them from leaving the Axis alliance.

Looks Like A Long, Hard Winter

—WEB.BROWN

DECEMBER 1942. Starting December 11, 1942, through December 31, 1942, boys who turned 18 since July 1st will register for the draft. After the first of the year, when a boy turns 18 he will report to his local draft board to register. Men aged 38 to 45 will now be deferred as long as they get essential jobs in farming or the defense industry. Desperate for men, the United States begins drafting men ages 18 and 19 in what was called the Boy Scout draft.

A Fresh Substitute Enters The Game

—WEB. BROWN.

The Winner And Still Champion

I'M COMIN' HOME NOW, MA!

711 DAYS IN SESSION

77TH CONGRESS

FATHER TIME.

—WEB. BROWN.

DECEMBER 17, 1942. The 77th US Congress wraps up its session with a record-breaking 711 days in session. In that time, they dealt with an array of legislation from neutrality to war.

A Tough Nut To Crack

—WEB.BROWN.

JANUARY 5, 1943. The Allies continue to battle General Rommel's forces in Tunisia, and the Desert Fox is not easy to defeat. Hitler will eventually evacuate his top general, but he angers Rommel by refusing to allow his troops to withdraw. Rommel sees letting his men get captured as a blunder and will eventually take part in the plot to kill Hitler in July 1944.

JANUARY 20, 1943. Reports that the Russians have lifted the siege of Leningrad are being published by the Associated Press. A Russian offensive helped opened up more supply lines to Leningrad, where many citizens were starving. Over half a million people had died during the siege which started September 1, 1941. The siege did not end for another year, but the increased supplies helped turn the tide.

Right In The Fuehrer's Face!

—WEB.BROWN.

JANUARY 27, 1943. President Roosevelt meets with Winston Churchill and America's Allied partners in a secret meeting in Casablanca, Morocco. The Allies discuss their war aims and announce for the first time that they will only accept an unconditional surrender form Germany, Italy, and Japan so that they can eliminate them as military threats to the world.

JANUARY 29, 1943. Americans and the world are still talking about the surprise meeting between Winston Churchill and President Roosevelt in Casablanca. Everyone is wondering if a date has been set for the invasion of Europe. American soldiers were shocked to get a visit from their President in Africa and Americans could not believe that President Roosevelt made such a long and dangerous journey.

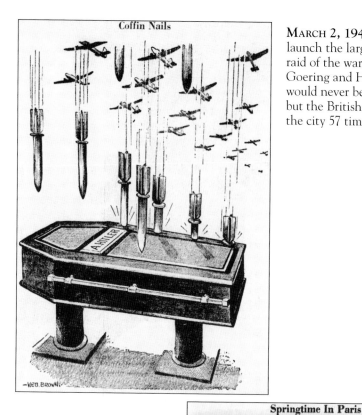

Coffin Nails

—WED. BROWN.

MARCH 2, 1943. The British launch the largest bombing raid of the war on Berlin. Goering and Hitler said Berlin would never be bombed, but the British have raided the city 57 times to date.

Springtime In Paris

APRIL 6, 1943. American B-17s begin to bomb Paris, or, as the *Beacon Journal* called it, the cafe of Europe. Oscar Wilde once said, "When good Americans die, they go to Paris." In World War II, the US Air Force changed Wilde's quote to "When good Americans fly, they go to Paris."

MAY 5, 1943. As victory in Africa nears, speculation mounts on where the lightning will strike next. Will it be Sicily, Italy, the Balkans, Southern France, Norway, Western France? Time will tell, but one thing is for sure: the Axis is on the run.

MAY 7, 1943. Families during World War II start to be torn apart. Mothers are heading off to war work, and fathers face being drafted. America was quickly running out of men after lowering the draft age at the end of 1942 from twenty to eighteen. Fathers were being drafted sporadically since 1940, but by the end of 1943 the primary people being drafted was fathers. Many of them died in combat in 1944 and 1945.

Busy, Adolf?

NAZI NEW ORDER

BOMBINGS

SET BACKS IN RUSSIA

TUNISIAN DEFEAT

INVASION THREATS

RIOTS IN GERMANY

UNDERGROUND ACTIVITY

WEB. BROWN

MAY 15, 1943. The war is not going well for Hitler. After losing Africa, he is faced with another invasion. The Germans are in retreat in Russia and continue to face bombings at home and underground activity everywhere. The agreement by the Allies of unconditional surrender means that once the war is over Hitler is through.

It's HIS Head

RUSSIAN STONE WALL

HITLER

JULY 7, 1943. Hitler launches his third offensive against Russia and the 1943 invasion is a week behind the failed 1942 invasion and two weeks behind the failed 1941 invasion. Hitler is gambling on knocking Russia out of the war before the Allies can invade France and start a western front. It is his last chance to conquer Russia as victory continues to slip away.

July 13, 1943. The Allies fight in the invasion of Sicily and Americans speculate where they will strike next. Mussolini jumped on the Hitler bandwagon after he saw his initial success in World War II. But the war has not helped him or the Italian people. It won't be long before Italy gets rid of him and asks for peace.

Only The Beginning

'When In Rome--'

July 20, 1943. General James Doolittle, the same man who led a bombing raid over Tokyo in 1942, leads 500 American bombers on a raid over Rome. The Allies had avoided bombing Rome due to its religious significance. After dropping leaflets to let the citizens know about the upcoming raid, the Allies bombed the city in daylight to destroy military targets.

Fiddlers Three

JULY 21, 1943. The Axis dream of world conquest is going up in flames. Sicily is falling into Allied hands, and Rome has been bombed in preparation for the invasion of Italy. The Nazi war industry continues to get battered by bombs, and daring raids on Japanese held areas continue. Speculation by the US Navy is that America may need to fight Japan until 1949.

JULY 23, 1943. Debate rages about the bombing of Rome. Everybody puts the blame where it belongs—with Mussolini and Hitler. Mussolini could evacuate his military personnel and let Rome be occupied. The Allies had been avoiding bombing Rome even though the city was contributing greatly to the Axis war machine which was causing the deaths of many Allied soldiers. The hope is that the Italian people will overthrow Mussolini.

In A Duce Of A Fix

JULY 26, 1943. Hitler is using the Italian forces to stall for time. He did it in North Africa, Sicily, and continues to do it in Italy. Mussolini has been overthrown, and the Italian army has yet to surrender. Hitler will continue to use Axis forces in Italy to stall the Allies while he tries desperately to find some way to win the war he is losing on every front.

Stalling For Time

Next?

JULY 27, 1943. Mussolini gets booted out of Italy, and his 22-year reign is over. The fascist dictator was the one who schooled Hitler, but it was Hitler who became the master. Mussolini took advantage of Hitler's rise to attack other countries like Ethiopia or invade France after he saw the Nazis closing in on Paris. Ever the opportunist, Mussolini chose the wrong side and lost.

95

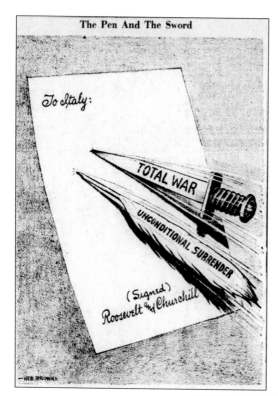

The Pen And The Sword

To Italy:

TOTAL WAR

UNCONDITIONAL SURRENDER

(Signed) Roosevelt and Churchill

—WEB.BROWN.

JULY 29, 1943. "Mussolini and his Fascist gang will be brought to book and punished for their crimes against humanity. No criminal will be allowed to escape by the expedient of 'resignation.' Our terms to Italy are still the same as our terms to Germany and Japan—unconditional surrender,'" said President Roosevelt to the *Akron Beacon Journal* from his fireside chat.

AUGUST 6, 1943. The Russians recaptured the heavily fortified city of Orel in another crushing blow to Hitler's hopes of victory. The radio out of Berlin spins their retreat at Orel as a planned evacuation. After 22 months of occupation, the Germans barely escaped the city as the advancing Russian army almost had them encircled.

Whose Plan?

TO OREL

TO BERLIN

IT'S ACCORDING TO PLAN!

RUSSIA

AUGUST 11, 1943. The Allies continue to hammer away at the Axis. The Russians are driving on Kharkov, Allied bombing on German industrial targets continue to take their toll, and the Axis armies are trapped and close to defeat in the Sicilian town of Mussina. President Roosevelt and Winston Churchill meet in Canada for their sixth conference to plan the next phase of the war.

Hammer And Tongs

Plenty Of Reason To Worry About The 'Overhead'

AUGUST 12, 1943. President Roosevelt and Winston Churchill meet and one topics of discussion will be the invasion of Western Europe. The question is, are the Allies strong enough yet and the Germans weak enough yet for the invasion of Europe to be pulled off without mass casualties?

OLD MAN RIVER—
He Don't Say Nothing; He Just Keeps Rolling Along

AUGUST 14, 1943. Stalin and his Red Army keep on rolling through the German army. The Russians have recently taken back Kharkov, Bryansk, and Smolensk. Experts are concerned that Churchill and Roosevelt are meeting too much without Stalin and are worried about what will happen after World War II. Signs of the postwar Cold War are there. Right now, though, Stalin is silently beating back the Germans.

AUGUST 19, 1943. The 8th Air Force went on its first mission on August 17, 1942. Since then, they have dropped 15,722 tons of bombs in 82 missions. The 8th has lost 419 bombers while destroying 1,728 fighter planes and damaging or possibly destroying 1,541 additional fighter planes. The 8th Air Force has learned a lot in its initial raids and is expected to bring total destruction to Germany.

Under It

SEPTEMBER 3, 1943. Allied raids over Berlin continue to escalate as General Hap Arnold hints that there are bigger bombers than the B-17 being made. General Arnold is hinting at the B-29, which primarily will be used to bring destruction, including the nuclear bomb to Japan.

SEPTEMBER 4, 1943. American and British forces invade Italy in an effort to knock the Italians out of the war. Hitler will lose his Axis partner. The Allies will gain a springboard to later invade Southern France or the Balkans. Allied bombers coming out of Italian air bases will bring more raids to France, Germany, Austria, and Czechoslovakia.

On Bended Knee

—WEB.BROWN.

SEPTEMBER 9, 1943. Italy surrenders and, as the *Akron Beacon Journal* put it, the Axis junior partner is on bended knee. The fighting isn't over, as Hitler has an estimated 10 to 15 divisions south of the Brenner Pass, and it is expected that the Germans will hold the heavily fortified areas in Northern Italy. Hitler is delaying his inevitable defeat and trying to buy more time by prolonging the fighting in Italy.

Sticking The Old Chin Out Again

—WEB.BROWN.

SEPTEMBER 16, 1943. Nazi paratroopers rescue Mussolini to set up a puppet fascist government in Italy. Mussolini answers to Hitler, and Germany hopes that Mussolini can create a civil war in Italy. The Italian people are unlikely to fight each other over the ousted dictator. Make no mistake about it: Mussolini's days are over.

SEPTEMBER 20, 1943.
Hitler once boasted that no one could penetrate fortress Europe if they tried to invade. President Roosevelt in a speech to congress famously highlighted that Hitler forgot to put a roof on his fortress. The Allies have air superiority and the Nazis are almost helpless against them.

SEPTEMBER 23, 1943.
Newspapers are reporting that they believe General George C. Marshall will be named Supreme Allied Commander to lead the invasion forces in France. Marshall distinguished himself in World War I and was once an aide to General Pershing. It was General Marshall that was selected by President Roosevelt in 1939 to build up the armed forces over 33 other senior generals. Coincidentally, it was General Pershing in 1918 who was the lone voice advocating for the unconditional surrender of Germany as he predicted the German war machine may rise again.

Halloween In Berlin

GHOSTS OF MILLIONS OF WAR VICTIMS

OCTOBER 28, 1943. Hitler and the rest of the Nazi war criminals will have to answer for the millions of war victims that have died as the result of their actions. There is nowhere to run or hide to escape the ghosts calling him.

NOVEMBER 2, 1943. Representatives from the United States, China, Great Britain, and Russia meet in Moscow. They agree to a postwar peace organization that will become the United Nations. They agree not to make a separate peace with Germany and to hold war criminals accountable for their actions. People are skeptical of Russia, and for good reason: Stalin will cease to be an ally after the war.

A Bigger And Better Headache For Der Fuehrer

HERMANN, MORE ASPIRIN!

UNITY AT MOSCOW

NAZIS RETREAT IN ITALY

U-BOATS FAILING

BALKANS SEETHING

BOMBERS STRIKE AGAIN 'ONE OF OUR CITIES IS MISSING'

WEB. BROWN

NOVEMBER 7, 1943. The government announces their worst kept secret, that the Army is constructing and will soon be raiding Japan with the new B-29 super bomber. The B-29 will extend America's bombing range and deliver destructive blows to the Japanese mainland on a consistent basis.

NOVEMBER 11, 1943. Armistice Day 1943 is celebrated, marking the 25th anniversary of the end of World War I. Immediately following World War I, Americans were disappointed in the Versailles Treaty. They felt that greed and pettiness ruined any hopes for a lasting peace agreement. Woodrow Wilson told Americans that they were fighting the war to end all wars, except it wasn't true. World War II, the most destructive war in history, was born out of World War I. This time the Allies are going all the way to Berlin and will not pull their punch.

Foolish Question No. 17,285

WOULD YOU CARE TO NEGOTIATE?

JANUARY 21, 1944. Reports of Germany trying to make a separate peace with Britain one week and Russia the next indicates Hitler is getting desperate. Retreating on the Eastern front and about to be invaded on the Western front, Hitler looks to loosen the noose around his neck. The Allies have pledged to not make a separate peace and experts think the Germans are concerned about having the Russian army in Germany after their brutal treatment of Russia earlier in the war.

Voices In The Night

WE SHALL HIT THEM AGAIN AND AGAIN

BERLIN

WHEN WILL THEY STOP?

FEBRUARY 17, 1944. Berlin has been hit with 15 heavy raids so far, and the last one was the biggest yet. A total of 2,800 tons of bombs were dropped in 20 minutes at a rate of 140 tons a minute. American and British forces have lost 3,366 bombers so far in European raids. The cost is deemed to be worth it, as these raids will save lives by shortening the war.

MARCH 17, 1944. The Nazis scramble to retreat in the Ukraine to avoid being trapped by the advancing Russian army. The Russians hope they can move fast enough to rout the enemy and capture large swaths of territory before the spring thaw brings mud and flooding that will slow down their advance.

Spring Harvest In The Ukraine

How Times Have Changed!

APRIL 12, 1944. Hitler and Mussolini used to make front page headlines that struck fear across the world. Nowadays, Hitler and Mussolini are garnering second-page headlines. The *Akron Beacon Journal* summed up their meeting eloquently: "The bogeymen have lost their power to frighten anyone. It's their turn to be frightened now."

An Omen As D Day Approaches

APRIL 13, 1944. The world waits for D-Day! It could be in a few days or weeks, but everyone knows D-Day is coming. The second front that will lead to victory with a march all the way to Berlin is near. D-Day will be one of the bloodiest days of the war, and casualties will skyrocket in Europe and the Pacific in the next year. The price for unconditional surrender is blood.

'Forward Into Battle'

JUNE 14, 1944. "Today the American flag is carrying this message of freedom to people all over the world. There is no room for oppression under the stars and stripes. On the beaches of France, in the ancient shadows of Rome, and in the Pacific Jungles the flag is carried forward against the enemy, a beacon of hope for the millions yet in slavery," reports the *Akron Beacon Journal.*

JUNE 20, 1944. The invasion at Normandy has been a success, and the Allies continue to gain ground. Winston Churchill was so happy with the success of the invasion that he predicted the war may end in the summer of 1944. Reporters immediately rebuked and criticized him for not being realistic and giving the war-weary millions of the world false hope.

Stranglehold

And They're Not Firecrackers, Adolf!

JULY 1, 1944. Hitler is surrounded by Allied firepower. The Germans are being bombed in Italy, Russia, and France. The German people themselves would provide another big boom on July 20, 1944, when they attempted and almost succeeded in assassinating Hitler with a bomb. The assassins hoped that ridding their country of Hitler would save Germany from destruction and Soviet occupation.

His Only Chance To Hide Away

JULY 5, 1944. Reports that Hitler is preparing to flee draw this response from the *Akron Beacon Journal* and cartoonist Web Brown: "No matter to what high mountain or distant shore Hitler may flee, he cannot escape. Unless, of course, he sees fit to send himself to the grave before some angry patriot or a stern court of international justice declares his life forfeited. There can be no safe hideaway for this murderer anywhere on the face of the earth."

A Difference

I'M JUST LEANING; **YOU'RE** FALLING!

JULY 25, 1944. Hitler looks poised to fall, five days after his own military tried to assassinate him. Hitler rounded up and executed thousands after the assassination attempt, as was his style. Whenever anyone challenged the Nazis, he responded with brutal violence and mass murder. The assassination attempt shows Hitler's days are numbered.

AUGUST 1, 1944. The Russians are outside of Warsaw, Poland, where Hitler started World War II on September 1, 1939. In August 1944, Hitler's on the march—in the wrong direction.

What A Difference Five Years Make

The Masterpiece Begins To Take Shape

AUGUST 9, 1944. The Allies, also known as the United Nations, meet in Washington to discuss the postwar world. The leaders from Russian, America, Britain, and China discuss creating a post–World War II organization to keep the peace. These four countries talk peace now and engage in a costly cold war after World War II.

Just One D-Day After Another

AUGUST 14, 1944. Web Brown turns out one of his most popular political cartoons of 1944. The summer of 1944 was not a good one for Hitler and Germany. The Nazis are already blaming the loss of the war on the Generals that tried to assassinate Hitler. Doomsday is coming, and Hitler is running out of time.

AUGUST 16, 1944. Charles Stanton's famous quote from July 4, 1917, when he spoke at the tomb of Marquis de Lafayette in Paris, France, was, "Lafayette, we are here." In World War I it meant that the Americans were here to help France win the war. In 1944 Web Brown references it as the Allies invade Southern France at the Riviera beaches.

Lafayette, We Are---

AUGUST 17, 1944. Hitler is being attacked on four fronts. The Allies are just 35 miles from Paris as they advance from the west and south in France. Churchill meets with Marshal Tito in Rome bringing speculation that the Allies might open up another front in the Balkans like they did in 1918.

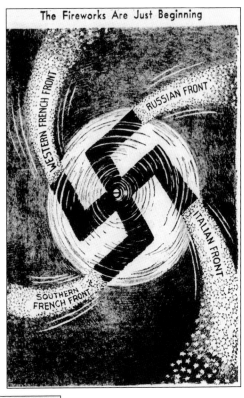

The Fireworks Are Just Beginning

WESTERN FRENCH FRONT

RUSSIAN FRONT

ITALIAN FRONT

SOUTHERN FRENCH FRONT

But Where?

THERE MUST BE SOME PLACE TO HIDE!

—NEB.BROWN.

AUGUST 21, 1944. Hitler continues his search for a hiding place. British field marshal Bernard Montgomery tells his troops that the end of the war is in sight. Hitler is not as close to defeat as Montgomery and others are predicting. September, October, and November 1944 will be bloody, and December 1944 will see Hitler launch a surprise winter offensive inflicting some of the highest casualties of the war. The staggering death toll will change the American motto of "Win the war in '44" to "Stay alive in '45."

To Arms, To Arms Ye Brave

—WEB BROWN.

AUGUST 24, 1944. The French underground did not wait for the Allied armies to arrive in Paris to come out and fight. Reports were that the French had started fighting against the Nazis as the Allies approached Paris. After four years of suffering under Nazi occupation, Paris falls back to its people.

Paris Fashions---1944

THIS ONE NEVER GROWS OUT OF STYLE!

FREEDOM

FRANCE

—WEB BROWN.

AUGUST 25, 1944. The Battle for Paris, which began August 19, 1944, is almost over as the Allies are reported to be taking the French capital. Reports are rolling in that the French people are celebrating in the streets even as there is still some fighting inside and immediately outside the city. The *Beacon Journal* suggests that French general Charles de Gaulle send Hitler a souvenir copy of *The Last Time I Saw Paris.*

AUGUST 31, 1944. A desperate Hitler hints at a secret weapon that he will unleash to help Germany win the war. The *Akron Beacon Journal* asks, "Have Nazi scientists found the atomic explosion that science fiction writers have been predicting for years? Is it possible a death ray has been perfected?"

SEPTEMBER 4, 1944. Americans work on Labor Day 1944. US workers answered the call both before and after Pearl Harbor, producing goods on an unimaginable scale to help win the war. Americans helped both Britain and Russia defend themselves against Hitler with much need aid. They also helped China defend itself against Japan. The American military has packed a potent punch from the start by using the muscle of American labor.

No Hiding Place Down There

THIS PLACE IS TOO GOOD FOR YOU!

SEPTEMBER 7, 1944. The world is getting reports from authentic sources of Nazi mass murder in the French village of Oradour-sur-Glane, of the Polish at Lublin, and at the Czechoslovakian village of Lidice. "No wonder Hitler and his gang refuse to give up, even though they are licked. They must know that an infuriated world will demand stern punishment for their crimes against humanity," reports the *Akron Beacon Journal*.

A Pledge To The Past And The Future

THE UNKNOWN SOLDIER 1918

THE HOPE FOR LASTING PEACE

UNITED NATIONS 1944

NOVEMBER 11, 1944. Armistice Day 1944 is celebrated with the hope for a lasting peace on everyone's minds. When the war ends, everyone wants what the World War I and II generations have fought for: peace.

114

NOVEMBER 12, 1944. President Roosevelt is elected to a historic fourth term as the president of the United States of America. In an overwhelming win for Roosevelt, America let its President know that they were ready for him to lead them to victory. Uncle Sam rides shotgun as FDR takes the country toward victory and peace.

NOVEMBER 15, 1944. Hitler has not been seen in public for a while, and reports out of Germany are that Heinrich Himmler, the head of the gestapo, has seized power. Hitler would disappear from the public eye from time to time, and after his own people tried to kill him in July of 1944 there was always speculation about him being overthrown or killed.

Pushed Back At Last

JANUARY 18, 1945. The Russians push the Nazis out of Warsaw, the capital of Poland. The Polish people suffered greatly during the Nazi occupation of their capital and country. The *Beacon Journal* summed it up: "Every atrocity, every cruelty that the warped Nazi mind could devise has been visited upon the poles."

In Unison: 'Many Happier Returns'

JANUARY 30, 1945. President Roosevelt celebrates his final birthday. Americans kept him in the White House for a fourth term to lead them to victory and a lasting peace. Roosevelt's death later in 1945 will be a blow to the peace effort. FDR won't be there to keep Stalin in line, deal with the Chinese Civil War, or to keep the French out of Vietnam.

FEBRUARY 2, 1945. Hitler finds a menacing shadow on Groundhog Day 1945 and is in for a long winter. The German winter offensive failed, as the Allies won the Battle of the Bulge. The Allies are speeding toward Berlin on the Eastern and Western fronts. Hitler and Germany won't last much longer.

MARCH 24, 1945. The world waits as the Allies move in for the kill. The first army is rolling after crossing the Rhine River, and General Patton's third army is, too. Marshal Bernard Montgomery has his British troops driving from the lower Rhine region, and the Russians continue their offensive in the East.

Running With The Ball

MARCH 27, 1945. The Allies are running right through the Nazis on their way to Berlin. Victory is in sight, and everyone wonders why the Germans don't give up when it's obvious they have no hope of winning. Casualties continue to mount in both the Pacific and European theaters, and April 1945 will bring more telegrams of death to American families.

TO ALL AMERICANS:

Carry On!

APRIL 13, 1945. America and the world is stunned as President Roosevelt dies. FDR passes the torch and Americans will carry on his dream of world peace and justice. FDR's death is a significant blow to the peace process. The Cold War followed World War II, with China becoming communist in 1949, the Korean War in 1950, and later Vietnam. Could Roosevelt have created a lasting peace? We will never know.

APRIL 17, 1945. Harry Truman speaks to the US Congress for the first time since being sworn in as president. The man who made headlines for walking to work on his first day in the White House lets the world know that his goals of unconditional surrender for Japan and Germany are the same as President Roosevelt's. President Truman says that the San Francisco Conference, which will establish the United Nations, is still going to take place in 1945.

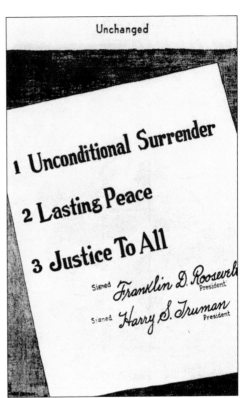

APRIL 28, 1945. The United States and Russian forces close in on Berlin from both sides and have their hands around Hitler's neck. Rather than surrender, Hitler will commit suicide April 30, 1945, by gunshot in Berlin.

Five

THE ALLIES DRIVE
TO VICTORY
MAY 8, 1945–NOVEMBER 21, 1945

A Flag Flies Over Germany

UNCONDITIONAL SURRENDER

GERMANY

MAY 8, 1945. V-E Day, short for Victory in Europe Day, arrives with the unconditional surrender of the German army. Americans celebrate the Allied victory, though most heed President Truman's advice and go about their normal day. The war with Japan is still not over and Americans are encouraged to save their celebrating for the unconditional surrender of Japanese forces.

MAY 9, 1945. America's celebration is short. After Berlin, their next goal is Tokyo. Though Japan has no hope of winning the war, especially now that their Allies are gone, experts warn it could take years to beat them. America must concentrate their efforts at home and abroad to speed Japan's defeat.

MAY 16, 1945. Now that the war in Europe is over, the Allies will go about the task of holding Nazi war criminals accountable for their crimes. Millions of war dead are the accusers as the world begins to learn more about the mass murder and other war crimes carried out by the Nazis throughout the war.

May 30, 1945. "There is one memorial that all of us must strive to create. Nothing could be more fitting. Nothing would make the souls of our departed heroes rest more peacefully. Permanent world peace would be the greatest 'living memorial' that could be erected to honor the men who have died in all wars," the *Akron Beacon Journal* editorialized on Memorial Day.

June 17, 1945. *Akron Beacon Journal* editor John S. Knight meets with President Harry S. Truman at the White House. Though very different from President Roosevelt, Truman has done well so far in his first two months as president of the United States. Truman has one goal, to be a good president. That sits well with every American citizen.

JUNE 26, 1945. Fifty nations that had been meeting in San Francisco for two months agree on the charter of the United Nations. The United Nations will be the peace organization to replace the League of Nations, which failed to prevent World War II. One main goal of the United Nations is to avoid World War III. The ability to create a lasting peace may rest with Great Britain, Russia, America, and China, who are Allies now—but not for long.

JULY 4, 1945. Americans have fought and won bloody battles in Luzon, Iwo Jima, and Okinawa and are marching steadily toward Japan. The fireworks have started but cost has been heavy; more American soldiers died between June 1, 1944, and May 31, 1945, than in any time period during the 20th century.

Open Door Policy

— WE.G. BROWN.

JULY 18, 1945. Admiral Halsey's naval fleet shells Japan's coastal industries and massive raids by hordes of American B-29s from Saipan are striking Japan daily. America is softening Japan for a coming invasion, destroying Japan's ability to wage war. America's fighting forces are exhausted with heavy casualties in 1944 and 1945 in Europe and the Pacific. Combined with a lack of manpower at home, President Truman will decide to use a destructive new weapon to end the war.

JULY 28, 1945. Japan rejects the Allies' surrender ultimatum and promises to prosecute the war to the bitter end. Americans think Japan will continue to be destroyed by bombing raids and finished off through a mainland invasion. No one knows that America has developed a nuclear bomb and is considering using it rather than continuing the bloody fighting.

Will He Grab It?

August 7, 1945. America drops the atomic bomb on Hiroshima, Japan. The nuclear bomb reported to be equal to twenty thousand tons of TNT is hard for the world to comprehend. Everyone is convinced that if there is a World War III, the world will not survive. Still, many hope the invention of such an awful weapon will discourage war and ensure peace.

August 8, 1945. The world holds the key to the future. Will they choose peace and prosperity for everyone or the destruction of mankind? The atom bomb is scary, and many people label it as evil. The hope is that mankind chooses to use atomic power for good things like cancer treatment and as an abundant power source to provide cheap electricity in abundance.

Sign On The Dotted Line!

SURRENDER TERMS
WE'LL BE GOOD

MACARTHUR

JAPAN

—WEB.BROWN.

SEPTEMBER 1, 1945. Japan formally surrenders on the USS *Missouri* in Tokyo Bay. General Douglas MacArthur is in charge of the Allied occupying forces. MacArthur and the Allies will successfully establish democracy in Japan that continues to thrive in the 21st century.

Sitting On The Lid

ATOMIC BOMB SECRET

OCTOBER 10, 1945. President Truman announces that he does not have to share any of the secrets of the atomic bomb with any other country except for the two countries that worked on it with America—Great Britain and Canada. Truman is essentially letting Russia know that he will not share any information regarding a nuclear weapon, though everyone knows it's only a matter of time before Russia figures it out.

OCTOBER 12, 1945. The United States is set to discharge more than a million soldiers. You can bet that these men, including some who have been overseas for more than two or three years, welcome the sight of the Statue of Liberty or the Golden Gate Bridge. Soldiers often say that homesickness can be worse than combat, so there is no doubt they are glad to be home.

Modern Christopher Columbus

MOST BEAUTIFUL LAND IN THE WORLD!

Justice Writes The Sequel

MEIN KAMPF
ADOLF HITLER

WAR CRIMINALS' TRIA

JUSTICE

NOVEMBER 21, 1945. The trial of former top Nazis as war criminals has begun. The list includes Goering, Hess, Schacht, Ribbentrop, Papen, and Streicher. There was no justice in Hitler's Germany or in the countries the Nazis occupied during the war. The first step in bringing justice back to Germany is holding these war criminals accountable.

Postscript

Web Brown, the man who started his career in 1899 after returning from the Spanish-American War, retires after 46 years of cartooning on Christmas Eve 1945. Throughout World War II, Web was at the top of his game and was one of the best cartoonists in America. It is fitting that Web, a veteran himself, retires at the end of World War II. Web fought on the home front, and his job is done. December 24, 1945.

The grave of Daniel Webster Brown and his first wife, Susan, in Glendale Cemetery. Web is buried in the family plot of his maternal grandparents along with his mom, who died when he was 18 months old. The Hardy family plot can be found in the middle of section 21 atop a hill overlooking downtown Akron. (Photograph courtesy of the author.)

Web Brown is pictured with legendary editor John S. Knight at the *Beacon Journal* 25-year dinner at the Sheraton in 1959. Of the 560 *Beacon Journal* employees, 119 had been with the newspaper for 25 years or more. Retired employees, like Web, often attended.

Web Brown is pictured here in his retirement photo in 1945. Web worked for 46 years from 1899 to 1945 after returning from the Spanish-American War. A daily cigar smoker, Web lived to age 98, dying on March 4, 1974. In his retirement, Web took up oil painting and gave away many of his portraits to local organizations and people.

About the Author

Born and raised in Akron, Ohio, Tim Carroll attended Akron Public Schools before obtaining a history degree from the University of Akron. Both of his grandfathers, John M. Carroll and John F. Ward, served in the Pacific during the war. He published his first book, *World War II Akron*, with The History Press in 2019. The author can be contacted for speaking engagements at timothycarroll27@gmail.com.